Snooker Poei

(2nd Edition)

George Stanworth

Illustrator

Mark Bennington

i

ISBN-13: 978-1981870608
ISBN-10: 1981870601

ii

POETRY FOR PEOPLE THAT DON'T NORMALLY BUY POETRY

CONTENTS

If I'd Picked Up A Snooker Cue

If I'd picked up a snooker cue, when I picked up a
pen;

and then gone on to build a break of eight or nine or
ten.

If I had only listened more to those who
understand;

who told me not to play the game by using just one
hand.

If I'd just watched Big Break much more, instead of
writing rhyme;

and studied Foulds and Knowles instead of Byron all
the time.

If I'd just gone and bought more chalk, and even used
a tip,

upon my cue, then thought perhaps to practice just a
bit.

If I had researched Virgo's words instead of Wilfred
Owen;

and written many papers on 'Where's The Cue Ball
Going?'

If I had only listened more to whispering
Ted Lowe

instead of sometimes listening to Pam Ayres in full
flow.

If I had studied Parrot's wit and Alex Higgins
Flair,

instead of Larkin, Betjeman, Wordsworth or John
Clare.

If only I'd heard Snooker Loopy played a little
more,

instead of writing verses that sometimes never
rhyme!

If I had just stayed up all night to watch the grinder 'Cliff',

and not penned many rewrites of Kipling's poem 'If!'

If I'd just seen the final frame in Nineteen Eighty Five,

and had a longer tape cassette which didn't then rewind.

If I'd thought of a funky name like Jimmy 'Whirlwind' White,

the 'Hurricane', or 'Rocket Ron' – perhaps like 'Dynamite!'

If I had done these things I've said, then yes, I really know it.

I would have been a snooker star, and not an unknown poet!

(Based on Rudyard Kipling's poem 'If')

Snooker

Snooker

Creative, Mathematical,

Potting, Plotting, Re-spotting,

Cues, Chalk, Theatre, Sheffield,

Inspiring, Welcoming, Accommodating,

Dramatic, Historical,

Crucible

If You Can't Be Great

If you can't be great, be rubbish,
and nothing in-between.
If you can't play like 'The Rocket'
then play like Mr Bean!

The Break-Off

At break-off time, you hear fresh air,
as everybody takes great care,
ensuring sounds do not escape.
(A bit like prayer time at a wake.)
There's silence, silence everywhere.

When cue strikes white, the white then scares,
the outer reds, who must prepare,
themselves for every tearful scrape -
at break-off time.

The melancholic reds all share
one final, futile, hopeless prayer,
and then await, await, await,
the impact of that cue ball quake.

The Welsh Wonder

A)

Mark's the Welsh wonder, a potting machine.
He's the greatest left hander that there's ever been.
He's the current world champ, on top of his game,
has twenty two ranking events to his name.
He's a coach now in SightRight and deems it a
dream,
and loves having banter on the Twitter scene.
Mark's the Welsh wonder, a potting machine.
He's the greatest left hander that there's ever been.

B)

He may not practice much these days,
but what a year he's had.
He's even been World Champion
after eating a kebab!
He's aiming for another,
as he carries on his reign,
but if he wins, then hopefully,
he won't strip off again!

The Triangle

I

could   have

been   in   an

or-   ches-   tra,   but

pre-   fer   snoo-   ker   more.

The Rocket

Ronnie's the rocket. The fastest we've seen.
His maximum break is the quickest there's been.
Still he keeps winning, whilst not slowing down.
This year he'll go for another world crown.
He's won 5 already, and when in top gear,
very few players can get very near.
His rivals are hoping he gets even faster,
so one day a frame will end in disaster,
and cushions and table all go up in flames,
due to his speed, so he forfeits the game!

I Potted A Long Red

I potted a long red and gave out a scream,
as it was the best shot that I'd ever seen.
Still needing 8 snookers, I hoped this would mean
the start of a comeback. (The best that there's been!)
I needed to focus, and not start to dream,
as my best ever break was only sixteen!
I potted the black and gave out a scream,
as I aimed for the green in the worst miss there's
been!

The Crucible

Sheffield hosts the greatest play,
which starts in April, ends in May.
A story over seventeen days
that wows and thrills in different ways.

Drama dances, stagecraft sings.
Tension twirls, emotion swings.
Critics comments swell the queues,
as sessions get 5 star reviews.

Players enter, players leave.
History in subplots weave.
Snooker is the best of all
for theatre that will enthral.

The King Of The Crucible

Hendry kept winning and winning and winning.
Seven times world champion. His rivals weren't
grinning.
His long pots were stunning. His pot success great.
Eleven times he made a maximum break.

Thirty six titles in ranking events.
He'd win with attack or win with defence.
A legend from Scotland with an MBE.
He's one of the greatest that there'll ever be.

The Trainee Ref

'One hundred and eighty!'
(I'd potted the black.)
The former darts scorer
was given the sack!

The Magician

He's called 'The Magician',
but he's not David Blaine.
He's just very tricky
to beat in a frame.

He conjures up pots
again and again.
He's not 'Penn or Teller'-
Shaun Murphy's the name!

The 1980 World Championship Final

Higgins

Hurricane, Quick,

Exciting, Entertaining, Inspiring,

Popular, Legend, Successful, Consistent,

Thinking, Evaluating, Defeating,

Slow, Grinder,

Thorburn

An Unfair Advantage

Twenty two balls, including the white
were all looking forward to our snooker night.
They dressed in their tux, all looking a sight,
but the cues on the night then all went on strike.

My mate (who had heard) was extremely slick,
buying replacements extremely quick.
His choice for himself was a broom, he weren't
thick,
as he purchased for me a snapped cocktail stick!

I Set Up A New Snooker Tour

I set up a new snooker tour
that Ronnie would not find a bore.
In mountains and hills,
there would be more thrills -
but after this trial I'm not sure.

Mark Selby

M ultiple world champion

A nd

R anking event

K araoke king.

S nookers required rarely stops this

E xceptional Jester from

L eicester

B eating

Y ou.

Pleasure

(A poem about the snooker shoot-out)

What is this frame if, time's so rare,
We have no time to stand and stare.

No time to see the perfect shot,
No time to think about the pot.

No time for banter with the crowd,
No Terry Griffiths thoughts allowed.

No time to think of ranking points,
or hear the creaking of our joints.

No time to think of safety play,
which makes the sport so great I'd say.

A poor frame this is if, time's so rare,
We have no time to stand and stare.

*(Based on the William Henry Davies poem
'Leisure')*

What Am I?

Dream-Catcher
Smile-Hatcher

Fist-Bumper
Joy-Jumper

Crowd-Cheerer
Ball-Clearer

Match-Shaker
Top-Breaker

Time-Framer
Life-Changer

What am I?

I am a 147 maximum break.

The Nugget

S ports personality.

T wenty

E ight.

V ictorious ranking

E vents.

D J

A lso.

V ery

I nteresting -

S eriously!

What Would Taylor Have Done?

I was losing eight nil and having no fun.
I thought to myself what would Taylor have done?
I kissed the big trophy as if I had won.
I lost eighteen nil to my ten year old son!

Commentator's Curse

Don't believe a commentator stating who will win.
Don't believe a commentator saying 'That's not in!'
Don't believe a commentator giving us their view.
Don't believe a commentator advising
'How to screw!'

Don't believe a commentator stating
'That won't pot.'
Don't believe a commentator's view on a golf shot.
Don't believe a commentator speaking any words,
for as soon as they say something then the opposite
occurs!

The Whirlwind

J ubiliant

I nfluence

M esmerising

M illions

Y early.

W hirlwind

H eights

I gnites

T otal

E ntertainment.

The Kick

I suffered a kick
when close to the win.
I don't think it's fair
when the ref kicks your shin.

I Potted The Colours

I potted the yellow
then potted the green.
The brown, blue and pink
went down like a dream.

I potted the black,
but my bubble soon burst,
as my mates said I needed
to pot some reds first!

Alan McManus

Alan McManus
is a great commentator
with superb insight.
His surname is tricky to
rhyme with though. Hence this Tanka.

You Aren't Out Of The Frame Just Yet

You need a snooker, coldly sweat.
But one good shot, and who can tell?
You aren't out of the frame just yet.

You view the table. Start to fret.
The balls are not positioned well.
You need a snooker, coldly sweat.

You play a shot you won't forget.
Applause goes up a decibel.
You aren't out of the frame just yet.

Your rival is the best you've met,
who seems to cast a different spell.
You need a snooker, coldly sweat.

You hit and hope, and play Roulette.
You're lucky, and your fans all yell:-
'You aren't out of the frame just yet.'

Your rival doesn't get upset
and aims as well as William Tell.
You need two snookers, coldly sweat.
But you aren't out of the frame – just yet.

Where's The Cue Ball Going?

It's gone for a stroll
down the hole
called
'Pocket Lane'
again.

Ding Junhui

D iscerning.

I ngenious.

N atural.

G ifted.

J oyful.

U nbelievable.

N oble.

H ero.

U nlucky.

I ncredible.

The Tap On The Table

It's polite
to like
exceptional play,
and tap the table,
or gesture
in some suitable way.
Inside though
you hate it
a lot,
and scarcely believe
your rival's managed
to play
such a shot!

The Century Break-Away

I tried a screw shot yesterday, but got it oh so wrong.
I ripped the cloth completely, and knew that before
long,
the owners would come over, have a scream and
cuss,
so I knew I'd better leg it on the next '100' bus!

John Parrott

A 'Parrott' once found snooker fame,
by being World Champ in the game.
On 'A Question Of Sport'
he never once squawked,
as he only was 'Parrott' by name.

It's Hard To Predict A Winner

When the 'Rocket's' on form, he's the player to beat,
but all of the others still strongly compete.
Most are World Champions, who are not content
making up numbers in every event.

There's Selby and Higgins and Williams and Ding.
Incredible players expecting to win.
There's Allen, Maguire and Bingham and Day.
Players who too can go all the way.

Robertson, Wilson, Trump and 'The Hawk.'
Multiple winners who all 'Walk The Walk.'
Carter and Murphy and Brecel as well.
Who's likely to win? – I just cannot tell.

This adds to the drama, the tension, the fun –
which is why I believe the sport's number one!

Shall I Compare Thee To A Snooker Break?

Shall I compare thee to a snooker break,
a safety shot, a Master's great?

Shall I compare thee to a foul stroke,
a miss, a kick, a Parrott joke?

Shall I compare thee to a fluky pot.
a plant, some chalk? I'd better not.

You hate the game,
don't feel the same,
(I'd end up in the shed again!)

(Based loosely on William Shakespeare's Sonnet 18)

Pre-Pre-Pre Qualifying School

There once was a player called 'Sloth,
who wouldn't have beaten a 'Moth.
He misjudged each shot,
and miscued a lot,
and ended up ripping the cloth!

The Final's Final Frame

There's adrenaline, excitement,
handshakes and applause.
You want to show you're confident,
whilst hiding all your flaws.

The break-off gives no chances.
You sit. You stand. You play.
You're waiting for the moment
the balls will fall your way.

You need to use the spider,
as well as the extension.
Your sleeve is near the yellow ball.
It all adds to the tension.

You pot the ball. You're on a break.
You're leading in the frame.
The next few shots are vital.
They could decide the game.

You miss the blue ball off its spot.
You think you got a kick.
Your rival gets the white ball cleaned,
and makes a forty quick.

He runs out of position.
His safety shot is poor.
You get out of your chair again
as all your close friends roar.

There's nervy shots and fluky shots.
There's screwing back and kisses.
The pressure you're both under
causes many fouls and misses.

The frame goes to the colours.
The tension is so high.
You need to pot the final black
to make sure it's a tie.

It's potted, so the final frame
will end on a re-spot.
Whoever pots the black this time
will go and win the lot.

The double that you try just fails.
Your rival should now win.
He doesn't hit the ball that well,
and the black just won't go in.

You know this is the moment.
This moment is all yours.
You pot the ball to win the match,
and take all the applause.

You go and give a handshake,
and then pump out your chest.
You go and lift the trophy,
knowing you're the best!

George Stanworth was born in Shropshire and has performed at numerous schools, libraries, and entertainment establishments across the UK.

George was a finalist in the 'Lyrics Only' section of the 2014 UK Songwriting Contest with his song 'The Wonder Of My Life'.

George's previous publications include:-

Darts Poems
Your Sax Is On Fire
A Floristry of Palpitations
Short Funny Love Poems
Don't Trick Or Treat A Lion
Christmas Poems For Children

www.georgestanworth.co.uk
gs1975@hotmail.co.uk

Printed in Great Britain
by Amazon